This book belongs to:

Made in the USA
Monee, IL
20 January 2022

89439069R00063